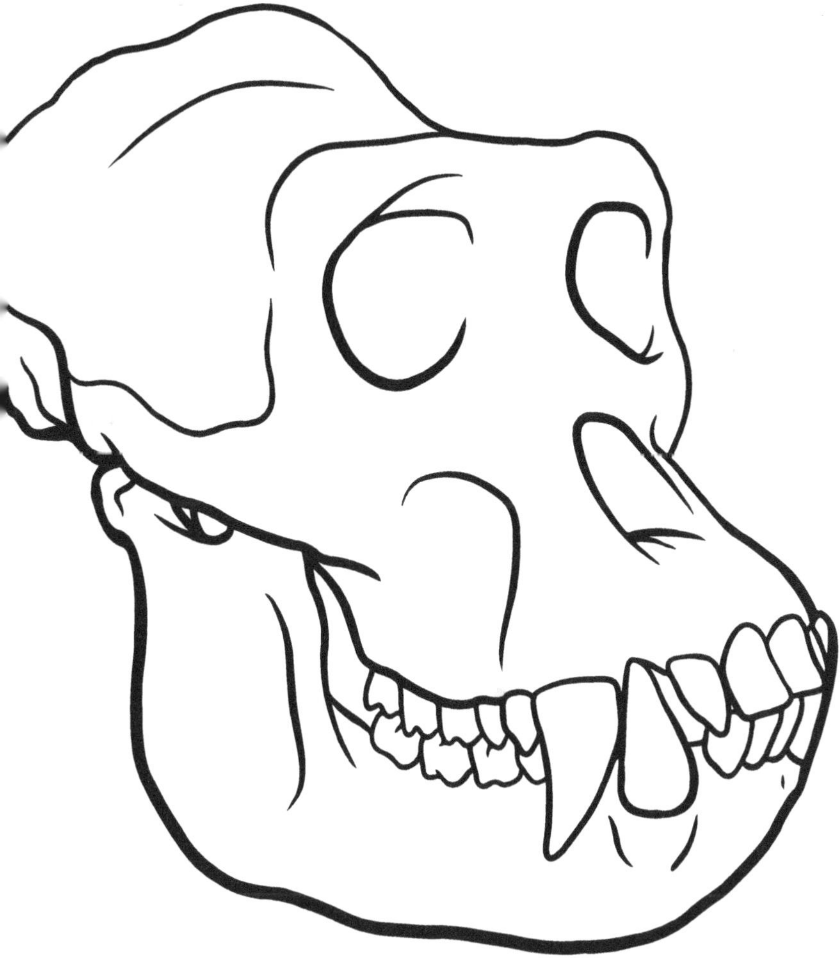

Also by SJ Fowler

SELECTED WORKS:

Come and See the Songs of Strange Days (Broken Sleep Books, 2021)
Sticker Poems (Trickhouse Press, 2021)
Bastard Poems (Steel Incisors 2021)
I Will Show You The Life of the Mind (Dostoyevsky Wannabe, 2020)
The Selected Scribbling and Scrawling of SJ Fowler (Zimzalla 2020)
Crayon Poems (Penteract Press, 2020)
Nemeses: the selected collaborations of SJ Fowler: II (HVTN Press, 2019)
Unfinished Memmoirs of a Hypocrit (Hesterglock Press, 2018)
I fear my best work behind me (Stranger Press, 2017)
The Guide to Being Bear Aware (Shearsman Books, 2017)
{Enthusiasm} (Test Centre, 2015)
Enemies: the selected collaborations of SJ Fowler (Penned in the Margins, 2013)
Fights (Veer Books, 2011)
Minimum Security Prison Dentistry (Anything Anymore Anywhere, 2011)

THE GREAT APES

Fowler

© 2022 S. J. Fowler. All rights reserved; no part of this book may be reproduced by any means without the publisher's permission.

ISBN: 978-1-915079-14-5

The author has asserted their right to be identified as the author of this Work in accordance with the Copyright, Designs and Patents Act 1988

Cover designed by Aaron Kent

Edited and typeset by Aaron Kent

Broken Sleep Books Ltd
Rhydwen,
Talgarreg,
SA44 4HB
Wales

Contents

chimp	9
gorilla	37
bonobo	59
orangutan	79
human	97

The Great Apes

SJ Fowler

chimp

A punishment for humans arrives divinely

in the apes.

Chimp don't hear.

Not the sun.

Always at the start of trouble.

Starting trouble for the sun.

Not hearing night.

Chimp only hears the de before the words that contain it.

It calms, chimp chews the wafer handed into its mouth that it was sposed to swallow.

Chimp don't swallow, chimp chews.

Chimp licks a bee like it was a battery.

First finger then middle then ring curls around the nape of the neck.

This is my enemy that was once friend

palm now on the jaw

now gun shot

no other life in the region of hearing can be heard

because palm now on the jaw

be careful a brave tree animal can be saying

get the car, says another.

I don't hear the sentence, I'm just watching

my role as a researcher is to watch

never to intervene.

But the fingers, the palm, the jaw.

Shadows are once hot wax being not so hot

The jaw of this other creature, this once friend now enemy is putrid.

Shakes, tears, calling in to rest no more rest, no more food

Food is blue.

Food is bland.

Food is tubed.

I wipe my orange juice from the carrots.

I hide my children. I barrel into my fence.

Someone else behind me, a human, will not stop talking.

Greasy ribs, electric wires, pearl jam songs, transmissions from the past they are obsessed with,

axes, tallow, beetle, belts, worn on badges, sharp planes.

Camera clicks, really? Now.

Chimp has got jaw for hot mess fear you utter.

Then guesses, a robber, who owns the most popular supermarket? Oh that's it.

Ecological concerns.

We're in the jungle mate. Chimp is elephant.

Chimp is war.

Chimp is noble.

Chimp is award.

Chimp hips are unimaginable to this liar sat behind me in its own fancy shit.

A sky fish will come I hope and tin looks facial features like birds knot themselves to distract

cardio from weights

nutrition from studies

evolution from pork

is it, think Chimp, the pork or the beans that got caught in your zipper?

Chimp drinks iodine and sweats it out for us to recognise it as close to us.

Knocking shoulders, eyebrows, chests. Never before ajaw.

Why did I research myself through Chimp?

No swimming here, no barons, no well to do at all.

The shop is closed, the food damp.

The elephants are cool but their babies rude.

They cross the laps of my girlfriend just to sit down and then where will she?

Where do you vacation? says from behind me.

Americans, I think, think and Chimp might jaw them.

But ugly finds itself.

Green military uniforms become suits

workplaces open,

roads bring transports, children sleep on them.

Phones are and will be.

I want to eat these trees to make the jungle the clear sight

and paper and a football field and a thing to keep me

as I want to live on and that kneeling throbbing

will last briefly

like the baby in the lap of my women

and it'll wink

and wince

and maybe even Chimp will see, look into my face,

keep its appointments

not leave me waiting for a text message.

Chimp, in being researched, will reveal

and the castle gate, famously locked,

will unlock and the smell will nauseaste

but you get used to it

because it is you, that smell

of kind of shit and armpits and infection

and why would the main thing be near the piss thing

so if you want to escape the open castle lock door

then its you whose weird

worried about things you can't change

Chimp, ruthless, will frightens boys

and teach with feathers

if you keep your distance

otherwise to teach with ripping

and biting

of limbs and cheeks and fury the likes of which

you'll only know about if you've had a war

or smoked and then died of voluntary melting cancer.

Breathe it, the key,

brand it, the fingerlock,

consume it, annoyed, young face, living clean.

The monster brains that eats balut, marrow, fish eyes, brains placenta,

bronze, gold, sliver and film.

Wine \/ rather I'd be a gorilla than a stage of denial

I can stop whenever I like.

I only do it for you've got to relax sometimes.

I like to eat on the altar, those foreign foods
.
That garden with the breaks, the red stones covered in roast meat.

Hungry Chimp is grabbing the enemies jaw though

not because of food

but because of anger?

No its raining a bit, the mush beneath our shared toes sways

and its not anger.

It's a crown you know the corona

radiata.

Road songs

the ability to read

the tasty pre frontal cortez

cortec

cortex

where you know yourself

can do menial labour with brooms or bricks

in immense existential pain bud get on with it we ain't paying you for nowt

that Chimp is nearly on?

Chimp Dolphin Elephant Octopus excetera

An arrow that all this reflection happens when Chimp takes jaw.

A limp passing before my eyes like a humming

unidefinitified

and ashamed at the lazy metaphor

and low grade thinking

and amateur psychologi

that led me here I am whispering into my foam

pity pity pity

show pity Chimp.

That thing feels too, like you, don't you?

Were Chimp a baker, or a gardener, removing loaves from earths

then I would be assured?

O look at the finger dexterity

the way it works the paddle

o the smells of it being fresh

it will do well in the market place and good on you I had such low expectations.

Neutral Chimp has a black chest

Ambivalent Chimp fanatical

Upper Chimp climbs

Vengeance Chimp in the midst

knows this moment of my approval pity

and crushes the jaw in hand

ripping teeth like aspirin in the belly of a suicide

A direct torpedo

A bad dance

A lover you don't want

A dying dog

A regret of self horror.

Chimp destroys the face of his fellow chimp,

crumples crushes the lower features of itself

folding in the other one known as Marc

into a faceless territory where the books say Good one, Good job

rather than History

where they say I told you

or You know this already

or Whatever

or Watch this

or Hold me

or Forget her

and Marc doesn't even die you know that

just has a lower teeth as a white chips with sauce

and a beard of pure black chest blood

and a lips of bad acoustic guitar songs in a locked room

and the tongue like a cheap sausage

but ripped up and stamped on

Nothing below Chimp hand has moved

it's a fight that's so still to refrigerator.

Cry, Mary, mother of glitter,

of suspicion

of spare rooms

of playing

of washing feet unnecessarily

of self-consciousness in the dark alone.

Weep for this creature that is your sons spasms in the aforementioned supermarket.

Back out, snuck out, strip, jump with bad legs.

Distorting Markk's face Chimp might be smiling.

But   what   is   a   Chimp   smile?

If not dying secrets.

Alone crying folds into ropes

with limps still on both apes until they become limbs

and cigarettes are wanted in my mouth despite the aforementioned cancer.

Audiences, I think, are spoiled brats.

Earnest aren't you?

Soft salad cream like balding creams

and nappies for adults who jerk

and stand up and stare and are rude.

I want them to be Mark instead

and does that mean I want Chimp to destroy their faces?

Mark what has become of thou\?

I should've listened to you

on the jungle floor when you gestured to me this might happen and

you can't breakfast Chimp

for he is unnamed

and you can't put a price on the innocence of that face

but I was blind

writing another poetry book no one but Mark will read

and falling into me mate's drug hole

and into a youtube music hole using easydownload.com to get those mp3s

and because Chimp is basically me

everyone keeps fucking going on about saying

we're two dnas apart

or something random in a paper so no one has to actually find out

but Chimp ain't my pal

not before the de-facing of Mark and not after neither.

Its mortally dangerous on the drag out because Chimp

still has Mark's facial

full held with bits of lips in the palm like a burning cup he's proving others it can hold.

Sing in synchronicity, read bibles, radio machines

imagine before emails

gulp property down

if you get a chance

because tomorrow you might be poison like Mark

collapsing hair like shit that everyone does

smelling your fingers after like Chimp.

O that's a good one

I'll get a haircut.

O it's broke his eyes too, Chimp has pulled his eyes off.

It's black moan.

That I thought was an idiot American before me

behind

was Mark's jaw death.

It wasn't a murmur but a moan of the end of a recognisable profile.

Give a dam, Chimp doesn't think.

Doesn't care.

You ever meant that?

Give me it back.

I once was able innocent to buy fancy drinks and despise people

who went on about New York as if it couldn't be predicted

or be a cesspool of morons

who basically all wished they were European.

Me, Mark insists

brandish becoming of my known last whereabouts.

Witness as a stupid academic word

clicks

milk this for one of your papers. Break in.

Reduce the vision to bad language.

Reach into the glass and make jelly.

Garlic, ejaculate, cream

the crushing of my face.

Stick tiny swords into the corners of my cheeks

that humans call dimples

until they age.

Flick up your umbrella, researcher.

Rock back and fore holding your knees.

Play a music on a techno.

Don't learn it.

Just do what suits.

Diamond this memory

memorialise

for it's all about you and what my kind

is your kind

in a timeline yours is to dispute.

Have a wank later, easy to move on.

Get me out of you and into me.

Steal my book from you and lend it back to me.

For I am to die with a gap in my face

where air will seep in like sea water

or stomach rumbling

that will not bleed right

but wind in

to obliviousness of my once friend now end

Chimp.

Mark.

You have taken an animal wire and snipped me off

like a religion.

I am yours in sorry, I'm ill. They grant me

enough to research

but not intervene.

Down, get down, was the advice. Duck.

I had make sure I survived to see, wherever this is.

The seeping.

Who knew Chimp would?

How could it deep red towers within all basic beheaving ever

been kept in the middle of the pink towel

and opened and looked at

to discern a disease

or a news pattern? How I fucking said, open your ears

are you tutting at me Kyle, I swear

I don't want you all belly and fat and screaming punishment kill Michael Kohlhaas

Kill the skies of lava with revenge on Churchill's mind

of that scene on the tube which ruined the whole movie

I've got nothing for you

you're a pig's head on the pitch

you're the career of cocaine not being specifically in holy texts

you're overthrowing as a thing, an art

you're contempt for the miracle of bottled water

you're forgetting organic was every food

you're crashing into the simple dirty rag

you're my ex wife who thought it gross I drank her period

you're the glowing mass which blinds children

you're the stupid enough to think you're cleverer

you're gunshots I said

you're saying one thing and doing other

the other is Mark

the other is diabolicial

what a word

you are judged judgement clapping its hands together and it ain't even cold

you are a twig giving away our position

you are what I am full of as Chimp looks up

drops Mark

and makes its way carefully over to the Wikipedia page about Pan Troglydytes to edit

some real info that won't need verification

for this is the one time the source can put up its own knowledge

for this is feet like hands

for this is Kyle crawling away from a scene that still has part of him

his body, maybe a cheek bit

or a fingers

or intestines bowels

for Kyle's great great great grandfather was scalped by first nations yea

he's scalped and messed with as he was dying

in a circle of native american

and american did it

whatever the context this has affected Kyle

that he's not allowed to feel angry about it

out loud

for this is the editors future

to realise the changes on wiki's endless sassy askance

for donations

that while you were worried about your mum's drinking

and what kind of poetry is going on

and AI

it was Chimp who landed on your shoulders

and stuck his middle fingers into your ears

like a medieval helmet covered in oliver oil

and made two fists and ripped yyyour ears off down

and as your hands came up to cup your lost ears

Chimp grabbed your fingers in a flower bunch

like it was the brakes on your fancy arrogant city bicycle for the green future

and squished them together with strength you didn't know

and then broke them back against themselves

and tried to pull them off

and partially succeeded

and put some of them in Chimp mouth

and chewed to spit them out like the aforementioned wafer

and then left it to see what your email that's just come is about

it's a mailing list you forgot signing up to

and an urge for you to check in for your upcoming flight to Berlin

but will you make that flight?

Chimp knows though not much and is now drinking your lynx body spray

is this enough of a topical issue for you?

is this massage?

and why did I not listen to Mark and stop it early before?

because jet set

because violin got auto corrected to violion

because I knelt on a bridge and wanted you to come on to me

and because you're so short and god I really loved that

I wanted to see sex then but I was scared and Chimp

vomited on the steps of the jungle at how far I'd got

my dick soaked by a different kind of rain

I have to wipe it all the time

it's scarred and it got stuck when I knelt over the bridge you were on

not half as scarred as a bonobo dick

and I looked about at you waiting and couldn't tell

what species you were even?

Vicious orangutan of the orange smoke veld

Skim gorilla of the wild bit, with the hair isn't shaved

Pygmy marmoset that never locks the lower door

Cocunut tree?

Fuck the pan?

Crawling mozart, with the crawling teeth?

I was like salt, like a hitting the wall with my teenage fists

and that throws hammers

so much hurt wow is it worth it?

The smug acid in my holding you instead of what I could've put in tinfoil.

Chimp knew then, was not ambivalent as aforementioned.

Chimp didn't think this as much

but poetically I'd say it was like

wake up speak and grab her she's willing

stuff yourself with salt so your face swells up and run

hit the wall if you want it doesn't matter human

no one believes you are doubtful because she's small

roll and forward and damp and ice your ears

but I didn't because you are well good

for that bit I knew

and Mark was in my ear

Mark the good one who looked after the orphan baby chimpanzees

who was followed around by kids

unlike me, with his ooo oo oooo ooouu huuhhh

which, I reckon, humaning his noises, into poetic words like

you're a mole it's ok to test the air with your nose she appreciates

you're a faithful monkey so sharp like a steak knives

you're an anteater off ants with a round mouth (he knows them personally)

you're afraid of die but you want too also so she's warm

you're that hole in the tunnel which is full of evil not yet

you're a show of unhappy but you know you well happy

you're nice to kneel bridges and watch and wish for

you're cocks wet and foiled in and scared and soul upset

you're presses against her steam a bit anyway wait a little bit more and I listened to Mark because of course

you were silk and you drew it

you were cheeks and intact, not even a hunt of biting

you were talented and asking me also

you were just two nights in a life of what 100000

you were frozen veins, uncuttable

you were better than me

you were dressing braids with stopovers and I saw it

which defeaned me to what Mark was actually saying

ouuuuuh uhhu hhhuuuuuu uuhuuuu

about Chimp for me to invent preventation

which I could done with my tranquiliser dart fun gun

because nukes and tech and duping

even when I'm a researcher whose career doesn't hinge on stupid apes

I say all the time they are well smart look at us

so I've got that dart with Chimp name on it

but Mark's encouragement made me maths

nightflights, meetings with people I hate, oldness

smooth young people when the aforementioned age

so I didn't also hear both at the same time

support and warning

now Mark has no lower face and is dying on the jungle floor

where he was born to Talula and Princess

and he was like a pea then, green ape of the baby boy

and he was kind like Kyle's wife

like that bouncer who let me in

like when my mum said goodbye to me just out with it and said I'm proud of you

like when I dreamt I had my own son

like when I didn't fuck everything into bulging dribbling shits

like when I cared what anyone thinks

like when before I go into A&E's without injury to watch others wait in pain

that was green pea baby Mark ape muscle

who grew up good with reserved power and aim

who welcomed us lazy research into the outer rim because

why not? Mark who gave it gladly for what he experienced

who saw those disappear into the recesses with grace and eternity as

a let alone let it go just leave it alone

a kitten even

Mark in the river fishing out a bag of drowning cats metaphorically

Mark who held back the sun and then made it come back

it's fine he growled and was celebrated because he wasn't disabled for his species Mark what? where?

unending stories that can't be

a base line presentation of a life you can't have

what glory in instinct was incredulous was about with him

he dies like a Mexican song in the mouths of the Dutch

he dies like a friend you well know you owe everything

he dies like a constant hushing from the gods timid rob sacredly

he dies like a shouting match drawed

he dies like guessing as a way out of trouble

he dies like we'll never be together really will we

he dies like a pensive fox who has no business in the jungle

he dies like a what I am doing with my life when your life is

he dies like a child being told they are an accident and liking that

he dies like a cold burger cooked again to ultravox veinna

he does like a shame taste for debauchery but half your age

he does like for us to all know it is never two colours

he does like a calendar of schemas that's all money work

he does like this means we're done and you don't even care

he does like buried as a meal in other floor creatures

he does like the puppies who did dig up their own parents bodies I saw it

he does like the man who bit me and who I tried to kill

he does like the cctv footage of what was done at our worst

he does like throw the first ston those who what was that?

he does like lyrics that remind of Mark that ape who was

he does like the blood of the face aforementioned slowly walking away

he does like the celebration of the violion that suctions airs

he does like the private chimp chamber that dogs baw

he does like passion seducing the tiny

he does for us like have you been proper ill?

he does for us like a swearword

he does for us like a European capital city overrun with lesbo shows

he does for us like a gym fart

he does for us like a hand still smelling of last night's cwisps

he does for us like traveloadge

he does for us like ironic use of claas A drugs

he does for us like warfilms that don't show the dying right he does for us like try to make it if you can but you won't try

he does for us like Knut Hamsun being half wrong

he does for us like hotel reception being offhand and fulfilling tripadvisor reviews

he does for us like a nervousness that comes out like rudety

he does for us like a name and a room number supplied to the gov't

he does for us like a confusing system that makes sense

he does for us like a bag of broth balls trying sausage

he does for us like an award's recent reputation

he does for us like the do your seatbelt sign now when you're into writing

he does for us like the you might if you would

if you could

if you were Chimpo

which you ain't

because Chimp is Chimpa

and that's the least of it

they don't have the time to watch other apes as though they could learn

can

a

chimp

be

immoral?

gorilla

No matter what you think

a divine punishment Gorilla starts early, returns

softly and nicely

natured in its most considerable aesthetic

back arch posturally fantastic

earths most supreme rage

under downy black furr

to the den, has an arrival time, eyebleed flight back to congo

subsequently a funeral

G   Orilla

anima pogrom

eyes naturally the croissants

thinks fellows are naïve to think anything is invisible

especially woman and mans

also supreme rage

but they hide it when the mountain apes

a terror deity made manifest

though polite they fear

not because he is a quick sweet beast quick he has power

no anyone has that with a gun

but because they know gorilla couldn't give a monkeys fuck

burst out crying

hold your hurt paw

well not a huge one for gorilla

but how they know how well he pretends compassion

to just get through the day

without conflict or slowing incident

especially travelling

come on over leave it out im massive

think they thinks gorilla

its peace

time

to throw your good self on the ground

squeeze cheeks

you say nothing when his jaw

wheel and deal, close locals due to rent raises

he'll go when he wants

not when you want

you said nothing

and what, when you did say, to bonobo, with his tongue out in the queue

did you accomplish? who are you?

can you be more marginal? less powerful?

where h\as your gl\ss eye rolled to?

who attends your birthday parties?

every been private?

every been twice?

wear loose fitting clothes? cover yourself with paint?

yea what have yyou achieved honestly with your speaking up?

go hold your water in your cupped hands sat in lotus

as Gorilla walks by with his beats

with his half suit hand cut and not that much more than off the wrack

with his Hitler bio under his armpit

with his ill slaughter you and then eat what's left

with his I wouldn't even need to yank

with his I eat liver and I positive vibe on bone marrow

with his I don't care if its partialaly horsemeat

with his you cant hurt my feelings no matter what you say

with his you ham cannot offend me ever ever

with his ill die of old age

with his I don't know what anxiety is

with his you fill the bowl's shape and in the past you'd be fine

with his Vienna and temporarily only in poor countries

with his newscycle is what does that mean?

with his restored self not needing a visa

with his murders but isn't a murderer

with his neither fascists or communists but knows what they are with his love of history

with his integration with his complex

with his absolute smell

with his grease

with his 1 star hygiene rating but regular custom

with his menu of organs

with his meat

with his shuddering orgasm

with his he knew Mark the Chimp would be killed by Chimp the Chimp

with his researching the watchers teenage years ago

with his business

can you enjoy bad things without feeling guilty?

Gorilla listens to music on a headphoned mp3 player

helps a human woman with her baby

helps an elderly woman with her walking

helps a waiter with a tip

turns music to appropriate volume to not tinny spread

covers his balls and dick with a sling of velvet

to protect the delicate sensibilities of the passenger

Gorilla sees make up, thinks yum

then thinks to see only the up being make, not at all pretty

but then it's identical early nothing is handsome

Gorilla can't believe a human man has such bad BO queueing

c'mon thinks Gorilla how can't you smell yourself? you ain't

just you in world you smell like a time of ratchets

and not the one we miss with beedays and the inopportunity

to wash but pre cultural ways when we all didn't crop

long view Gorilla has made something of something

the first Ape to wear pants has hand up in class

the majority were washed by their mothers but not Gorilla

partied and washing oneself while opening

gates filling them with come

ringing bells to varnish steps to slip monkeys

for apes invite the centaur comparison, they are legs like you won't believe

sinking ouuuooouuuu I'm going to come don't stop is Gorilla

I've corporated shouts rillgoa

Gorilla means status coming means guitar smash

Gorilla means polished shoes mean disturbed rib noise

Gorilla means float means accents that are putdownable

Gorilla means not what turns you on means what turns on you

Gorilla means drinking from skulls means double jump double bash

Gorilla means buddies with Cara Delevigne means whip whip

Gorilla means unopened letters means obey obey

Gorilla means darkness penetrada means lovely thunder boy

Gorilla means cribs with air con means chains you can stretch

Gorilla means perfume that murders means flesh castle with fur

Gorilla means a pack of dawgs means licking cliteroris' perfect aim

Gorilla means I could fucking you but I choose not to power

Gorilla means I know you couldn't do anything to me unless I let you power

Gorilla means you won't even see it coming power

Gorilla means it's still there while you make custard power

Gorilla means ghosts ain't real but spine crack is

Gorilla means Americos in Vietnam means Anglaise in Boer

Gorilla means cool hate means don't need to bother mate

Gorilla means pianos of salt means out the window then

Gorilla means if you don't like it means leave

Gorilla means monsters in the parasol means shadow dance

Gorilla means metaphorical impale means multiplying orbital bones

Gorilla means all the water is gone means push ups in minutes not numbers

So on the airplane Gorilla is heaven, is sweet something

taking up nearly two seats

is an addition noticeable to the otherwise indifferent staff

which is lady dominated who appreciate his pouch

but are intrigued politely to see what is within

what a beast of note

what a driver with ironed shirts

what a master plan

what a pining for the terrible dark possibilities they ain't done what a frightening spool

what generations of forgotten knowledge

what opinions on things they have not read a word about

but heard, heard Gorilla, who just nods

offering a soft ououuooouu

and maybe enormous hands open assisting with putting

a bag in the overheard compartments with such dexterity

even the BO man cleans his pits there and then

this is my coalmine knowing Gorilla

researching on now a gov't grant

given by Lee who also saw Gorilla in the streets and thought

like I, we need to interview this one to know

to know

how we go back through Pan Troglydytes and into

Homo Sapiens when it was better

which was in the previous line of time when it was better

so says Lee so funds Lee so watch I

Gorilla the dark young fresh king met me at a Lebanese

and shared muhammara as though it were free

Lee who reminds Gorilla of Mark

who will be used up by the power

who will be a corporate cog

in the empire of coins

in the poke of umbrella thinking

in the web of powers

in the reign of information

let's echo let's exchange let me learn

the agreement to fight the enemy was made

with living Lee in the restaurants of Antwerp

Gorilla is ape boss

and says an ingenious device for obtaining profit

without individual

because who wants that? least those who says it

at least Gorilla admit

says expenses are for Training my dogs

are for Burn the ships

are for Prudery the worse kind of avarice

are for the curse of our age

are for even the strangest aberrations as no cure for boredom

are for jollies

are for almost all our misfortunes

are for wrong notions we have about the things that happen to us

are for to know apes thoroughly

are for judge events sanely

are for a great step towards happiness.

are for his heart three or four times less sensitive

are for three or four times as much power of reason

are for what you call hard-heartedness.

are for refuge in having paid mistresses

are for more

are for great the scandal, reputation and brilliance

are for beauty as nothing other than the promise of happiness.

are for poising the water supply

] but everyone drinks bottled water anyway

did work fall into water?

did you make the case that work was bad, and go whole hog?

this is a gorilla sleeping on a plane

two seats for one

opening its mouth just below your feet, willing

the gorilla dreams of mines

sewn deep into the earth

stroking men down in those seams, coughing

massaging their neckes

paying for their passion, their warmth

their boy shouldering weight of goods

their enormous ping poing relaxation they requested

their juke bo

their muffs

the gorilla snorts at the part of the dream where the mountain

snorts

and coughs cocaine

into the anus of the petrified enemy

that lights it up

and builds pillars of salt to beard

the dawn like scenery

the gorilla sees eyes less black than its own

and nods

and the mountains below pukes vomit

grey and white and uncut all over the planette

those underground workers have eyes that begin to blind

eventually slowly dripping out

and gorilla has a new coat

that's why it steps away

invents flight

to apex predate

to fire the fire bowling strikes every lane

the gorilla dreams of televised debates

of asking why, like socrato

but why do you think

people are this why?

well, maybe, you, maybe, oou, maybe, never escape

underfloor heating of mite is rite

if I can then I can

what is now before me will soon be behind me

and no one every went poor underestimating the intelligence

of others

and those who aren't listening

unless you talking about them

maybe possible vision of backbiting or subtle digs

nah, insult by omission dreams gorilla

the giant pool of children of copious business doctors from farms o the world liberal of hurt

how mortificare is the confrontations that disrupt

and fail the testing water

that shows them unable to swim

while the caps melt seas even greater

grander does gorilla dream of a water logged future

smiling lips of the primate megashine

sleeping? tucked in

pragmatic philios

capitalism is nature rousseau

thanks calvin gorilla (& hobbes)

the the gorilla dreams of restocking toiletries

loves shower gels

their smells

washing up tide pods

to feed teens like Lee

that's why you dream of the gorilla's dream you freak

fresh fur king

who boils the eyes of your daddy

until you grow weird

and unappreciated

the researcher narrator knows

the tree of labour is leafy still

despite all your pointless theory

the acid of gorilla terror king reigns like a million

fire ants marching past the mines

and into lungs of friendly creatures

asking did you film us I'd love to watch that again

without recklessnesss gorilla has his drink repoured even deeply asleep

imagine being that muscular

thinks the air stewardess

imagine being that thin dreams the gorilla

to let something own

as a concept

a pure pinch

never cold

never hungry

imagine wanting to fuck but not being able to

right there and then

do the theorists of the miner's children no longer abide?

are they all celibates?

if so, the animal is damned

to extinction

a funny little laugh in gorilla's sleep

if not, what a fine line

to be so unbodily

and then need it from time to time

imagine how unsexy they are, the doctors

the gorilla (dreaming) kills the neighbour

pulls on his own balls

doesn't get off (saving for later)

rattles a tin

gouges out a tiny family in every city

smaller even than a sylvanian family

and then checks its balance

big numbers

numbers is just an age after all

wine and cheese to the discount stickets

enough numbers that they spell out

go hard or go home

what a decent lad, whispers that air stewardess

into her memo audio pad in her latest x8 gorilla phone

and the plane lands

and stairs dick out all cogged

and gorilla pads down first of the bellies

home

snakes breathe in the trees

mice talk business to traps

sleep wakes itself

cows piss their milk

valleys fill

worms see

crowns weigh

a door knocks

straight into plunder meetings

who did we scratch and who needs water?

and how much, Lee marmoset, lucky to have this role?

keep them lean and treat them bean

who built the bridge of aluminan?

who bribes?

briebes my fave thinks gorilla well rested

he's home to the land of a nod to the rumble

don't you look other way

it's there but do you know the feeling of the palm to palm?

it's delicious like the entrails of bird cooked just right

the calf liver all ripe and warm

the cheery rice of cherry

no matter what you think

the body is an object

even if a guerilla is not

even if a being is not

even if a atmosphere is not

even if a mood is not

even if

How did Gorilla begin becoming

C

E

O

I know you are desperate for narrative

so

he began as drug dealer

the arms dealer

deutsche bank

dealing

politics

imaginary gesaffelstein video

illuminato

revenge of the right on

the day is his enemy

down get down

kneel shits

then calmed down

businesses

is a need to love out the energy within

try it

before you buy it

bribe me reader

to answer the big one

was Gorilla ever born?

or come from a divine egg?

the answer is Gorilla got idea for bottled water

in the womb

and went from there one step at a time setting goals

ape eyes on prize

can

a

gorilla

be

corrupt?

bonobo

How would you know

you can't hear it coming

and Bonobo becomes pervert through history

for while you infer

you're also not one

because inside your sticky ribs

is space

without the need for a mix up

a

con

fus

ion

a chemical table of nightmare squires

whipping the sun

out of predictable slime

not a mask in sight

not a rock to chip

not a chimp to fear

the building was erected when you arrived

a flea favours the same areas

as a lover

here is a book maker for heretics

one can hardly imagine in what diversity

an ape can develop their debaucheries

all they need is a permissive partner in crimes who can set down in detail those things

when the imagination ape is inflamed, however great is variety

in all other passions, it is greater here, the abberations of this way

shall we distinction between that which is imagined and that is done?

nah, they can be the same in VR and if you try hard enough

sober science catalogues text us into perversions too

we had a good time didn't we?

fastidious in the bathroom, dirty in the bedroom? welcome to town

we had a good run did we not

oi toad nimbus

oi rubicon rose

oi hunger child

oi ribbon oven

oi effect and cause

oi cork eyes

oi gas mask

oi glue stick

don't pretend to Bonobo

bo's on time

bon's not acceptable stereotypes

bono's with your daughter she's fine having fun even

bonob's hangs your head in ignomy

bonobo's a circular artery

or a square field

or in denial

Bonobo is not your pathetic girlfriend boyfriend

Bonobo is not your excuse

Bonobo is not simplicity for the limited capacity

Bonobo is mysterious blanket of wanting to do things

Bonobo is Cordelia before all the bother

Bonobo attains the sea bomb wetness of your root

it is 1488 and cardinal is sniffing the arse

of his dog

o clement supermother

and it is 1677 and the marquis de sade is writing

what you thinking

because he is an ape aristocrat shaved just right

to get in history

and bonobo is reading this and thinking I am tame

compared to homosap ingenuity

and bonobo is rereading this and getting erect

while columns are being written about microhappenings

his Bonobo is being

grown up

and babies and other catastrophes

and the perversions next door, the wanking at the desk

and desire for a throat to be grabbed

and a face to be slapped

while the columns like line letters that say

how could the slapping?

I mean really could all the children not be named after fish?

rakhist

I mean really Bonobo need pull out his dick reading marquis de sade

but it's a Bonobo causality

we see what Bonoboes and expect Bonobo

but with homosaps no pattern to follow

not war war war war war war war war ware and such

so lets expect no more mean words in the heart black

with fear and pain and desire for escape

from the expanding chasm of blackened bonefinger death

the ruin of us all

but no connection here we different but all the same

unlike Bonobo who is

and is on to the next page to finish off politely into a leaf

and here's the rub

has no regret and is just reading on.

Pan

paniscus

is bread in the oven

is fluting

is recasting the lead due to contract disputes

and is aware of its passion aggression towards the producer

because they called the bonobo pygmy chimpanzee and less often, the dwarf or gracile chimpanzee

and made allusive reference to bonobo being endangered great ape

and one of the genus Pan

and so contract dispute isn't it

because why would I do you the favour?

long legs are relative, pink lips valuable,

a face attractable and what a tail-tuft through adulthood

this is why it got the lead

cutting for the role

now Bonobo parts long hair on its head

and asks are you looking forward to sensitivity?

are you feeling something?

in   ter   es   ting ??

Bonoobo likes to eat ass as the americans say

because why not have a wafer chew like a catholic?

"Quirky" redirects here. For other uses, see Quirky (disambiguation).

"Wacky" redirects here. For other uses, see Wacky (disambiguation).

Bonoobo introduce this to the casual dating scene

Why not where building up to later but now?

where no baby can be made

so Bonoobo turns pooper on the homospa

by having boatloads of anal course with its own hair and abs just one rule for Bonobbo

don't fuck your famille

without being demonstrably maladaptive

not including distant cousins course

From Medieval Latin eccentricus

derived from Greek ekkentros, "out of the center"

a neologism in 1551 when Bonobo was Congo

an astronomical term

a circle in which the earth, sun, deviates from its centre

there's no harm there's enthusiasm

See also

Byronic hero

Eight Eccentrics of Yangzhou

Individualism

Normality (behavior)

Personality psychology

Thinking outside the box

All this quality is why Bonobo has its highly successful acting school

to help apes

and all animals for matter

to prevent further hardship to the common creature

against the bloodsuckers who hover close ready to profit from every disaster

the parasitic other ape

Gorilla buoy unfriended

lapping the last drop of blood which falls

villains unjusticed

indeed

the lot of them

the entirety

who never so much as dream of a virtue

but actualy regard all virtues as Bonobo would prone to regard vice

jealous? because Bonobo is splendid moral as beautiful

weighing such, arms and legs were so strong

shoulders broad and powerful like chest, slim waist, beach ready

buttocks meaty

handsome black eyelashes, a straight nose

porcelain chompers that never bite

these splendors and a working penis

that could ejaculate eleven times in one calendar day

were not these envious uprights pure complaining evil

because of Bonobo activity?

impire deplorable

penchat for crime contempt

foul looking hairless-ish

bordered the maniacal

prudish hunched opposite

cruel scared shit eating

motherfuckers symbolically

pathetic self-hearted

a calumn of endless profusion of murder

and then hated Bonobo for licentiousness

the judgemental

pompous

condemnatory

hypocritical

humans

sure, bonobo had been seen on a sexvideotape, leaked into the internet

1. sex

and maybs

2. enticing a wonobo to let ejaculate on her hair on the top of her head

sure, also, other videos, showing bonobo

3. having a wonobo piss on his groin, clothed

sure, also,=

4. sucking snot from a wonobo's noise

5. teaching a wonobo mutual masturbation out of sync

6. having wonobo kneel on shoulders while he wacks

7. being impotent with wonobo

8. having logos

9. pulling down underwear from behind while wonobo kneel on chair and being disappointed it so clean and shaved like a child?

10. touching himself with wonobo sweater while she dressing

11. wonobo scratching his behind with red sharp nails

12. sniffing rear

13. sucking gentle on breasts

14. following fashion with wonobo by covering her in blankets

15. women with legs on two different separate chairs over bonobo

16. being spat on in mouth

17. being with older women

18. talking women into life of sin many thousands over

19. watching another monkey sex with monkey while women with bonobo

20. voyeurse

21. outdoor with women putting it in and saying its in now with women nods

22. with two wonobo, at once

23. pretending to be pimp in pre-agreed role play

24. watching football during intercourse totnam v eveton

25. sperming in a fancy dish

26. asking women to do hot yoga then licking her sweat up off

27. cleaning up in case someone else finds out

28. smelling armpits of own wonobo then women

29. damaged by nature or by the effects of law as qualify as suitable partner for bonobo to carefully lovemake but it's a condition

30. covering women mouth then sucking air from her burps

31. getting women to vomit up with his dick

32. translucent red ghost over wonobo while boning its memory

33. (28a?) eating up that women vomit with pleasure

34. swallowing women gas after giving her legumes (earlier in day, long video)

35. asking is women menstruating and then when affirmative answer really so happy about that and drinking it down dribbles to chin and all over dragon face

36. eating a placenta while jerking off

37. eating the discharge of that was in the bolt of the women with yeast infection

38. chewing soggy bread the women had just been eating!

39. trying to shoot his come into mouth of wonobo from distance as oral target

40. supine women

41. waiting for women to go to toilet and then that's the time to try it on?

42. onto food, but without too much motion

43. women on ladder wonobo gives milk aenema and inevitably drinks it as it comes out

44. women rubbing his body, otherwise known as Massage

45. pushes women bathroom inside where his comes from wow

46. chews the skin or else

47. being distantly with wonobo eyes thinking of elsewere? or someone other?

48. chewing nails after fingering women ass and eating shit a bit but not stopping with facial show of happy ccident

49. using contraceptive to thwart nature gods plan

50. (49a) using anal a lot to do the above

51. being able to get permission from animals because Bonobo speaks horse or crocodile or octo say and like egyptians, originary americans, having sex with them after a frank chat about expectations

52. having ballskin pricked with a golden needle

53. a whip used then the handle stuffed inside

54. a selective collective humiliations that begin verbally

55. a knotty stic pluned a few inches into the urethral canal rattled

56. being consoled after failue

alcohol and lemon in a cut made on the forearm

57. taking a sex worker to a funeral home in process not a funeral

58. goats

59. undermining confidence in the vain

60. using the fluids of another as lubricant on the dry for sexing

61. no one but an ape who is to be married the following afternoon

62. devirginating two on a day one of each

63. saying love to convince and not meaning it and leaving quietly

64. only nuns priests etc all voluntarily or any really religious

65. a of half age legal and double age on same day

66. honey yoghurt eczema boilingwax meats

67. Japanese wicker spinning cradle but its not in its an actual octopuss

68. hallucinogenic drugs as well as uppers and downers and drink and pharma from the GP at once and then hot

69. only those with criminal records custodial

70. ejaculating into a coffin

71. incest for real though cousin is fine

72. making a new one

O but then

pornography

Bonobo need not imagination anny longer for

its just there

typing

infinite acts

the end of lists

the end of innovative in the workshop

the end of culture of improv

the end of perversions

and in three months

but all is unsatisfactifying

no? eventually…

we are to it

just like Lot, imbued with such respect for holy

Bonobo wins divinity through emulating

the madness of Pygmalion

no longer surpises you surely?

was it not necessary in the beginning so as to populate the earth

with bolobos?

and something that was not an evil then

can surely not have become one since?

a pretty boon is not allowed

tempt Bomoboi just because he made the mistake

of bringing it into this world?

a mistake apes are

kin to make

did Bonobo choose its will

to urge?

you think so don't you

and makes Bonobos final pervato

    74.   love with righteous in the darkest sin

can

a

bonobo

be

depraved?

orangutan

Youth waste

it is sharp

but living is too short to be wide

but how did you learn to be so sick?

says the invested higher being

ape

the magnificent orango

learned tang

you have named

all

well, like old jewish books that have been unmemorised

like travellers we love in the mind but not in person

tell us how to end this horrible nightmare

force us into a improved submission

where we learn to accept the providence that eats

the other stuff as metaphor

for funny naff distractions

for no orangutan ever put their hand up to offer an opinion

and no orangutan claimed

sought, beckoned, beasted

it sits with a base so firm one would not move to attempt

life

unlived

when it is

you might as well stay because you won't eventually be able to

smile? the big boy

is overhead all apart from love

orangutan won't fight, say what you like

it won't be had

a wingspan stands before insult

though orangutan whispers to his followers

monkeys, dogs, frogs

even respected by Chimp, Gorilla, Bonobo

the insult is the humans best invention

and has a right laugh

but the other animals don't understand

for mystery lies within the parasites

its why orangu will swallow us

a brown eyed clarity that shapes wings

to organise

and this has always been the truth

what you seek

deforestation as metaphor for death itself

the kind of creature who invents the word confused

for the sensation of being stumped

rather than being confused

what is the difference between that which invents the word

that is the feeling,

and that which feels the feeling?

a big transformation

orangutan   >   you

a big distance happier than before

a big core not rubbing it in

a big sore right on the mind

a big red crown of youth

a big red voice of reason

a big red crop of rubber

a big red diamond lost on

a yellow beach

a big red fresh fruit

a big red spoiled brat done good like buddha

a big red not every twat saying they're out of time

a big red love without loss

a big red beauty as the promise of happiness

a big red repetition that is new

a big red guide, translated into german, but not

a big red understanding after soaked experience

a big red keeping it to itself steeped in books

a big red onion anti-moan

o professeur

and at the pear feet of orangit are sat

all (most other apes)

Here is the summa respectable and deservedly praised

here is a book maker for the faithful

one can hardly imagine in what diversity

a himo sapien can develop their corruptions, oran says

all they need is a dishonest animal in crimes who can set down in aspect those things

when the fancy is inflamed, however grand is variability

in all other desires, it is greater here, the aberrations of this way

shall we division between that which is fictional and that is done?

orangutan holds his eyes covered

the howler monkey screams it's not real

orangi nods gently

we had a good time didn't we?

every other being nods back

demanding in the bedroom, dull in the living room?

welcome to earth

we had a decent run did we not?

separate love from sex because of time aging

human concept

infers the eyebrows of the orange divinity

deity as much as well might be

O-Tang says come on de Sade was no more a moiderer than he was a coprophile or coprophage

it would probable in fact in fact be true to say

with carbon gas to be a trink

he preserved his sanity and succeeded in resisting his murderous impulses

by 'abreacting' them through projection upon imaginary villains

and here everyone laughed, everyone

after all, says the big O

did not goethe say nihil humani a me alienum puto

say what says a golden tamarind

for sake

there is no crime of which I do not feel myself capable

o yea cover version

sure says the orange and begins nibbing

every inch the ape priestess

every inch the healing blanket

every inch the good bet

every inch the panic room

cosy

brain damage

cte deconnecting

every inch every one's dreams are the same

every inch unspecial individuation

every inch the hirsuite harmonious

every inch the tetragrammaton

every inch the not advertising

every inch the ant keeper

every inch the fermes hrismegistus

every inch the orange hashem

every inch the placeholder for "O"/"U" vowel

every inch patristic apocrypha

every inch knowing you're in the comment section when you scroll and see a bunch of comments

every inch the sweatpatch yeti

every inch your best friend who never let you down

every inch non addictive drugs

every inch a mobile network operator

every inch occurring between red and yellow in the visible spectrum every inch the not thinking beyond anything

only ever undone by love

one weekness

by the coconspirator of bloods

wallet size pains of longing

lips harden to warn orangutan but not even with this one red ape

a rude fiancée

                there will be no more new ideas

so unjustloy beautiful seeming stepped from pages

rearranging all orangutan's body chemicals

as endochrine glands going stuttering pituitary

often getting out of weights way

such beauty often hardens trying at what is being done

whatever deadlift

the callousness of double helix impressions

with no hope of smelling sheets

sects of misted cocaine in ventilation of clarity

how does the world become traversed with protection?

without muscl?

there cannot be nostalgia when orang you tans

the animal house of friends gathers

to listen

imagine

with ears

and O R A N

G U T

A N

speakers

> "if I speak in the tongues of men or of angels, but do not have love, I am only a resounding gong or a clanging symbol"

speaks some more

> "no special significance should be attached to the name
>
> a disagreeable sensation in the pit of stomach is not entitled to be taken for compassion
>
> never be born or die in hospital
>
> one is no longer capable of something that one used to be capable of
>
> all cultural censors were bad at maths at school
>
> younger people have always noticed moral stupidity in everyone but themselves

by the time we reach years of fulfilment we have forgotten all about it and are far from wishing to be reminded of it

old moral notions, simply unendurable, come back

a slippery creature has tried to overwhelm in sleep, a belly soft, tender

there is no example of inevitability that can compare with the sight of a gifted youth narrowing down into an ordinary elder

an artist of real integrity must abstain from creation altogether

the long and the short of it is, there is no important idea that stupidity does not know how to make use of

something one craves for just as naturally as one craves for bread or water is, after a time, unnatural

one hears it laughing, turns around swiftly and looks into a face that is round and unmoving as a hole in the ground where a mouse has just disappeared

if mankind could dream collectively, it would dream manslaughter

stupidly profound, exciting sensation, touching immediately on the self, that one had when sniffing at one's own skin

tremendous energy into doing the very unnecessary this could be said about all of us today

there is another country where one is at home, where everything one does is innocent.

spend the rest of life in the conviction that although perhaps everything ought to be different, there is certainly no point in thinking about it

a second infinity is unfolding, in the course of which the constellations go on their predestined cycles, without his being in the world at all

one thinks it, feels it, has premonitions of it all the time, naturally, in the most various kinds of surrogates and according to one's temperament

for only fools, the mentally deranged, and people with idees fixed, can endure unceasingly

every act and its opposite are accompanied by the subtlest intellectual arguments, with which can both defend them and condemn them

the teachings of the inspired crumble into dust in the rationality of the uninspired, crumble into contradiction and nonsense;

are great ordeals the privilege of great personalities?

the baroque of the void walks upright

It is simply my conviction that thinking is an institution all on its own, and real life is another one

it often happens that brothers and sisters loathe each other in a manner far in excess of anything that could possibly be justified by the facts

thank goodness there are still some people who are capable of believing in simple things, in spite of having great experience but youth ends abruptly for orangut

but pongo is not sui generis

but the magic mandrake root more beautiful than a telegraphed picture

but to have eaten of one's mother's heart

but to to understand the language of birds

but to be more beautiful than an animal psychologist's study of the expressive values

but we have gained in terms of reality and lost in terms of the dream

but two weeks later the love ape had already been mistress for a fortnight

but this is the most menacing riff in history

but I listen this every day just in case I get murdered

but the bewildered solitude where all others lives exist a hundredfold

but the orange ape needs no sex

but the utan is sage not the herb

but

but the greatest ape is in love

you were already in the mind so repeatedly

and then you had to send that heart

the first in a series of projects

about death lives in love

in the ruin

of the ape

orange

phosphorus

named

Balthus

orange

juice

what is leaked from the eyes that see

such beauty

and is not aloud to murmur

I saw you, colour

I saw a blood red

like a feather from a sure thing

like organ blood from the mawkish who die for love

but them bettered

orangutan sees too in his loves

a restorative beauty that all else hurts less to

such appearance that regrowth happens

like a stemcell clinic of the chest

love needs just a night

a surprise

a constant noise

orangutan love is going to have to

as though its new

as though a red fur beyond the orange

where penetration hits the wall

again x again

what eros holds under dark

red saints bleeding

slipping finally exhausting

washed under a small

tap a noise of the lamb

a long slow farewell

a final grunt after all that work

white peaches in brown teeth

numb hands the size of hopes

blood orange on lips all about the body

seriously, stop

the orangutan will die of love and you'll wish

you knew how that felt

can

an

orangutan

be

too

shrewd?

human

a mystery

on the ape's face

as it limped from the primordial

juice

was resurrection

restlessness

a story about a story

a yellow pallor

a fat head

an erectus

a warm patch

a mimosa of thundrs

a raised by fire

a high on farming

a desired lesson

a school as a wacky fixe

a goat head rockhard

a cunning motherfucker

a petty conceit to get through it

a nice juicey bone

was to be had

was the gleam of the city

was the civil ise

the ape straightened its spine

and then immediately leant on the haft of its sword

and the weakness in its limbs

showed all other creatures

and altogether else that perceived, long dead nowadays

that despite the cold puddle behind it

the appe was to be spend 10000 years

sweating

out

what had taken it but a minute to acquire

nature / being

perceptions

selv

awarenesses

walking tottered suffering on two feet

"creativity" as a seminar for survival

beneath a natural gate

from a cave

which asked

is this really an ape? I thought you were forever

to make free with your pike?

a cock joke this early, rolled the dinosaur?

what the bloody hell is this massive weapon?

it protects us

splits us homidiae from the pan pongo interface

not hobbling with your weapon for a walking stick

how stupid you look upright

the dignify ape's eye brows

suggest as to whether it was there

or someplace else

presence was a pretty good clue

I am here

and out of the hospital

of origins

comes I

I

one slant line down

which skeletons language forever

poetry

and entirely everything else also

cooking, gardening, warring, computing

confined for love as robust medication with remorse

how strong it is we are yet to know

not stout enough to stand in the light too long

the sun burns

heathen earth

glad in misadventures harsher and more than anything you ever heard

in other creatures born days

taking up the invitation to travel

with intension to educate, to improve raw morals

that is the sole objective of this ape as an alive anecdote

apes imbued with the great peril

that perpetually dogs the footsteps

of that which permits themselves everything

while satisfying its desires

it may be forgiven the monstrous details

while pretending it didn't need to do

to be more

thriving

than anything that has ever been

rare that everything should be harmoniously organised

in one animal

the only skin to be a perfect companion

to chronesthesia

to autonesis

how like humans to be so gold

how like humans to mental time travel

how like humans to pretend it cares

how like humans to attach immense importance to avstract thought an nd language

how like humans to whisper see you in hell

how like humans to see their intelligence as distinct and not part of a continuum

how like humans to warn others of what it fears

how like humans to not recognise the sheer numbers and biomass of termites

how like humans to pretend it's blue when it's brown

how like humans to lean upon offcuts

how like humans to be thinking of its shopping

how like humans to think what it is doing is pointless

how like humans to think what it is doing is priceless

how like humans to touch arms appropriately

how like humans to expose nature to questions

how like humans to wake in a hard exoskeleton

how like humans to create umwelt

how like humans to be rolling dung into a ball

how like humans to pretend it is robot

how like humans to be collectively referred

how like humans to think metaphor is meaning

how like humans to let us down so often

how like humans to pick scabs and eat them

how like humans to tranche

how like humans to work out ecological niches

how like humans to pretend it is not attracted

how like humans to imagine it is good

how like humans to burn matter for motion

how like humans to try

how like humans to be late

how like humans to be an organ of a vascular town

how like humans to not believe in extrasensory perception

how like humans to not keep its arm between the armrests

how like humans to flow

how like humans to not know it has blinding odour

how like humans to blur its photography

how like humans to be on Instagram while writing

how like humans to have stereoscopic vision grasping hands the abolity to climb

how like humans to be erotic art

how like humans to wonder about the universe of which it is part

how like humans to be the principal lateral appendage of the aquatic
how like humans to conquer the seas

how like humans to miss its mum

how like humans to wobble

how like humans to dance, both in, and out, of the breeze

how like humans to terraform the weak earth to raise crops and not be hungry anymore

how like humans to specialise, academically

how like humans to like guns

how like humans to call a viola a violin

how like humans to get match funding

how like humans to overcook a steak

how like humans to be flattened and borne above ground

how like humans to misjudge the length

how like humans to need to blush

how like humans to take the absence of evidence as evidence of absense

how like humans to enjoy more that it might've bored people than pleased them because it bores itself

how like humans to be so patient, like Job

how like humans to chuckle

how like humans to moan

how like humans to quote shakespeare

how like humans to earn its fee

how like humans to call its tributaries daughters

how like humans to compare itself to everything

how like humans to own property upon which other waters work

how like humans to bloom like a flower

how like humans to let its own shape be born of it, to let it not owe its formation to anyone how like humans to read

how like humans to have a distinctive upper surface amassed with boats

how like humans to love and admit it

how like humans to have a distinctive lower mudded surface full of treasure

how like humans to hate and enjoy it

how like humans to scorch, yellow or darken its waves and wilt

how like humans to be separated from its source by abscission

how like humans to stop talking now

how like humans to have to say thank you in order to denote the end

to bring opulence to life on mud

to cry like baby dragons watching the sacred machine

lackeys of an evaporating deity

whose got funny teeth

who ensures

favoured by nature? fortune refuses

fortune showers? nature maltreats

and the erectus articulates oh yea

the hand of earth demonstrates the law of equilibrium

is the foremost law of the universe

governed all events of vegetable and animal

until agronomy, taxonomy, gastronomy until anomy,

bionomy, anatomy,

until economy, dichotomy, sodomy

nomenclature of at once the horoor and the muracle of nature

classification and irganisation of the ludic

woman and man does

formerly jelly-boned slimy belly-wriggling invertebrates

formerly miserable sodding rotters

formerly flaming sods

formerly snivelling, dribbling, palsied, pulseless

now grew into enchanted apes that gossip

apes who not think too much lest it inhibit unoriginality

apes the legless who teach running

apes like eunuchs in a harem, who know how it's done, who seen it done every day, but who're unable to do it

apes who salt up as many penguins as they find

veiled apes

apes who flatter themselves

apes in the eyes of their own lunar sea

apes who sweet talk until their lips numb

apes who stay, or burn the boats

apes who brag and swagger offer and promise

apes who settle down

apes who ready and willing

apes who ladyfy luck

apes who brain their groins

apes who ministrate to obfuscate and transmute base intentions

apes who were meant to be

apes who loan

apes who poke

apes who silvertongue to butter up and then run down

apes who invent seppuku

apes who keep fighting in the jungle

apes who absquatulate with beautiful chains

apes who sin through despair

apes who dance in closed rooms to let off steam

apes who never rain but pour

apes who dose of their own medicine

apes who match poverty with honour

apes who use trees to hang

apes who use dogs to watch

apes who use horses to drive

apes who use fish to bathe

apes who use birds to hover

apes who use sharks to film

apes who use cows to tap

apes who use sheep to war

apes who use bears to love

apes who use cats to hate

apes who use god to guess

apes who dare say a word against us

apes who look like monkeys

apes who make faces like monkeys

apes whose bloody faces look ugly like monkeys, when they cry, like monkeys

apes who come with faces ugly like monkeys

apes who orgasm with bloody faces like ugly monkeys

apes who presume reason

apes who create divine apes who know knowledge

apes who are all tantalus

apes who slay their offspring with affluence

apes who

apes who tantrum

apes who entomb

apes who derange

apes who kiss the devils ass

apes who shit and bury it

apes who die and bury it

apes who fuck and bury it

apes who birth and bury it

apes who invent the insult

fully erect

bipedal evil

plumb skeletons

on their segways

taking pictures

of purest laughter

apes who don't just speak, but talk

as though they could even think

can

a

human

being

be

meek?

Ape Out Your Unrest

www.ingramcontent.com/pod-product-compliance
Lightning Source LLC
Chambersburg PA
CBHW051656040426
42446CB00009B/1167